WHAT PEOPLE ARE SAYING ABOUT

MADE IT THRU THE RAIN

The author displays an incredibly deep understanding of the personal and devastating journey of depression. It offers empathy as well as direction to those people struggling with those demons as well as some useful strategies and inspirational quotes. Above all it has the ability to hope to those who feel hopeless from someone who truly does know how it feels.
Maggie Davies, Lead Therapist in Aneurin Bevan Health Board

I couldn't stop reading the book: the text bowls along and retains interest. I particularly enjoyed the use of poems and how the book has been structured. I recognized what you the author was saying and thought the condition was presented fairly, positively and with care.
Sarah Russell, Writing Editing Consultancy
(www.sarahrussellwriting.co.uk

Made It
Thru The Rain

The author courageously demonstrates
how an ordinary life can become
extraordinary and how experience
can indeed be the greatest gift

Depression isn't a sign of weakness...it's a sign
you've been strong for too long ...
Author Unknown

Made It
Thru The Rain

The author courageously demonstrates
how an ordinary life can become
extraordinary and how experience
can indeed be the greatest gift

Beverley Jones

**PSYCHE
BOOKS**

Winchester, UK
Washington, USA

First published by Psyche Books, 2012
Psyche Books is an imprint of John Hunt Publishing Ltd., Laurel House, Station Approach,
Alresford, Hants, SO24 9JH, UK
office1@jhpbooks.net
www.johnhuntpublishing.com
www.psyche-books.com

For distributor details and how to order please visit the 'Ordering' section on our website.

Text copyright: Beverley Jones 2011

ISBN: 978 1 78099 392 8

A CIP catalogue record for this book is available from the British Library.

Design: Stuart Davies

Printed in the USA by Edwards Brothers Malloy

We operate a distinctive and ethical publishing philosophy in all
areas of our business, from our global network of authors to
production and worldwide distribution.

CONTENTS

'Made it Thru the Rain' is dedicated to my precious
Mum and Dad
Who truly are my best friends
Thank you for your endless support, love and light

Foreword

I feel privileged to have been asked by Beverley to write the foreword to her book. I am very proud to have Beverley as one of the Sue Stone Foundation accredited coaches. Beverley has been on an incredible transformational journey, suffering depression and suicidal thoughts to living the wonderfully positive and fulfilled life she does now. She thrives at what she does because she has learnt the best way, I believe, through personal experience. Beverley truly walks her talk.

In *Made It Thru The Rain* she recounts her years of depression and explains what she went through and her darkest innermost thoughts and fears. This is the dark illness of depression that so many people suffer from. I found myself becoming excited reading about the things she did towards beating her depression, her challenges and successes and her passion now to help others. The last chapters are devoted to simple yet hugely effective tips and techniques to help beat depression and other mental health issues. This book is a wonderful read for people who are suffering with depression, their family members and friends, or just simply for a greater understanding of this subject.

Sue Stone

Acknowledgements

A big thank you to those who supported, inspired me and helped me through my dark days of depression. To name each and everyone would take a book in itself, a fact in itself of which, I am truly grateful.

There are those who held my hand every step of the way, there are those who, in the middle of the night took my calls and shone a light, there are those who listened and those who would advise. I had many who planned days out for me to ensure that I had a purpose, knowing that if they didn't I would resort to a duvet day.

There are those that knew and understood as they had travelled the same road and those who held me when I cried.

Each one of my close family and friends circle will know who you are and I thank you from the bottom of my heart.

There are my doctors and my counsellors who have my heartfelt sincere gratitude always for their support, guidance and belief in me.

I would like to express thanks to those who supported my business idea and assisted me with the name, the design and its message, the journey continues! Thank you to my publisher O-Books who through the publication of my story are helping me to assist and inspire others.

Thank you to the lovely Sue Stone for her generous spirit and her continuing belief and support.

And to Mike, thank you for always being there.

I wish you all a happy and positive life!

Preface

How do you recognise you are depressed? Since suffering from anxiety and depression in 2009 - my annus horribilis - I realise back then I didn't know the answer. However today I am a little more awake to it.

We all have bad days and for eighteen months prior to being diagnosed I had many of them. And that's exactly what I put them down to - bad days.

When the hours of crying became more frequent than the hours of not, you'd think I would've noticed. When the usual everyday tasks became too much, you'd think I would've noticed. When I started to suffer paranoia and panic attacks, you'd think I would've noticed. When I started to comfort eat, you'd think I would've noticed. When I became insecure and my confidence dropped, you'd think I would've noticed. And when I visited my doctor more in three months than I had in the previous three years, you'd think I would've noticed.

But no; and from a number of people I spoke to at the time, my behaviour had become the norm so they didn't recognise the signs either.

My usual positive self had been taken over and replaced by a negative, critical self. My self-confidence plummeted as my work and relationships suffered.

At the time none of this was recognisable to me. I felt I'd changed but if anybody commented on it I would deny it and refuse to discuss it. I felt like I was being personally attacked and I would spend my time alone sobbing and wondering why people no longer understood me. What was wrong with everybody?

As things got worse I would say to those nearest to me, 'I'm sure I'm ill. What's wrong with me?' It was always explained as, 'You're tired.' 'You do too much.' 'You worry about nothing.' 'It will all be better soon.'

If only.

It didn't get better - it got oh so much worse!

For those out there reading this who suffer depression, or for those living with a depressed person, I'm sure this will resonate - it may even make sense. At the time it didn't make sense to me or those closest to me.

It does now.

This is the story of my journey. You will read about my deepest fears, feelings and pain but through it all I *'Made it Thru the Rain'*.

Beverley Jones

Duvet Days

Get out from under the duvet!
I CAN'T!
Yes I could yesterday and
Yes maybe tomorrow I will
But today I CAN'T
Please don't ask me why
I have no answers
Just leave me be.

Chapter 1

How did I get here? Life, that's how. My journey has brought me to the duvet and its snug, warm hold that today surrounds me. My duvet days are just the best.

It's while I'm here that I feel safe. Safe away from the world, away from the noise that constantly, continually fills and echoes inside my head. It's like I'm living with a volcano sat inside me, just waiting to erupt.

I try to battle my thoughts. I don't want to think because it causes chaos: irrational thoughts that appear real, dark thoughts that appear to envelop my senses. I can't see, I can't hear, I can't taste and I can't feel. The only sense that is prevalent is smell. And why? Because I smell fear.

I'm so afraid I'm shouting, but there's no one around to hear. When I'm in company no one can hear my cries because silent cries can't be heard. It's a nightmare and I'm living it.

I've cried so much today my eyes hurt; surely there can't be any more tears? The only way to stop them is to sleep. Today I know it's bad because I woke myself up crying.

Doing daily chores has become impossible - everyone gets in my way and on my nerves. Just go away world, I can't be bothered with you.

It was following another duvet day that I took myself to the doctors. I'll always be grateful for the medical help I received from that day on.

I didn't talk at the doctors. I cried... and I cried... and just for good measure I cried some more. This brought on a panic attack and out came my inhaler.

The doctor's view: 'You have two weeks left before you are hospitalized. You need to take time off work to rest and recuperate. This has to happen as of today. If you don't... Well, the choice is yours.'

I saw that I had no choice. I finally realised that giving in was not giving up, and that in order to get my health and my personal well-being back on track I had to take his advice and take time off work.

Walking out of the doctor's felt like walking out on a life I had known for so long. Looking back over the previous two years I realised all the physical ailments I'd succumbed to were my body's way of telling me to WAKE UP!

I'd suffered an unidentified problem with my foot and ended up in a cast. I'd endured colds, headaches, sore throats and repeated kidney infections. During the first five months of 2009, I'd taken three courses of antibiotics, all for various infections. My immune system was shot, physically I was worn out and mentally I'd been crushed.

Burnout at its best. The doctor was right: I had no choice. I was on the point of collapse.

I'd always been a strong, positive person, always there in a crisis. I was a person who strove to do well and to always be there for others in all areas of my life. I wasn't important to me. I spent my life caring, sharing and helping; nothing was too much trouble. I seemed to have more hours in the day than anyone else so nothing was a problem.

Only it was and I hadn't told anybody. What had happened? I just got tired.

Tired, weary, teary and sad, that's what I'd become. It's a job now to say which emotion hurt the most, although looking back I believe it was the anger, which was a result of these emotions, that drove me to get help.

I got angry with me. *How stupid! How pathetic! How ridiculous!* What was happening to me?

I got angry with others: 'Can't you see I'm ill? Why can't you help? AARGH, LEAVE ME ALONE - no don't go, I can't stand my own company!'

It was the anger that drove me to cry the most. I screamed

when no one was listening. I shouted when no one could hear. I held my arms so tightly they would bleed. To shut out the constant noise in my head I would hold it so hard that blood would appear where my nails had dug in - that's anger and frustration at its worst. At the time, in my mind, this was the only way to deal with the internal screaming. My thought process shouted: *By making myself bleed I will hurt myself more than anyone or anything ever can.*

What crazy thoughts...

Listen to the story that your heart and mind are telling you

Just Listen

If you are willing to listen
I will tell
You may not like what I say
But listen and you may learn
The pain will be easier for us both
If you try to understand
I just can't snap out of it ...

Chapter 2

As I'd been forced to listen to myself, I now had what seemed like a huge, daunting task: I had to tell others.

How?

Telling others is so difficult. For me it felt as if I was admitting failure. I felt useless and pathetic. How could someone so strong, so able and so resilient, suddenly be this crying, de-energized, angry, negative person?

I'd been confident and courageous; now I was weak and scared. In my mind I tried to tell myself it was a phase that I would quickly get over. In my heart I knew I was lying to myself.

It was probably the bravest thing I'd ever done in my life, even though at the time it felt like the most cowardly. I stood there and freely opened myself up to the world - scars and all.

I told family, friends and colleagues I was suffering a breakdown, that the strong person they had known needed rest. I poured it all out. There was no more hiding, no more pretending. If I couldn't admit it to myself and those closest to me, I knew I would never recover and become the real, true me again.

There were those who were patient, those who tried to understand and those who, quite frankly, didn't have a clue. In fact, I would go as far as to say, some didn't even believe me.

I now had to set about a very unfamiliar journey. I couldn't cope anymore: not with work, not with general situations like food shopping, socializing or communicating. In fact, I just couldn't cope with life.

Life was hard work. Getting up was tough some days; in fact, when I made it to the settee in the lounge to watch TV I was so proud of myself, what a break through! I understand that moving from the bed and its snug duvet to watch TV all day in the lounge in my dressing gown may not seem like an achievement, but I can tell you, to me it was like I'd climbed a mountain. I couldn't talk to anyone, either because I had nothing to say, or I would just break down in tears. Looking back, I realise that while I felt I was on a lonesome journey, I was in fact surrounded by those closest to me who were travelling the road with me.

There are a number of those closest to me who have admitted to crying tears for me because it hurt them to see my sadness. I was blind to this at the time and, to be honest, it wouldn't have made any difference anyway as I was totally oblivious of other people's feelings. Depression makes you selfish, but you don't see it. The only world that matters is yours, and that's because, quite frankly, you believe that there is no other world outside of it.

The hurt in their eyes was so hard to bear at times because, try as I might, I couldn't change where I was. I was in pain but it was a pain in the mind that I thought only I could feel. Those closest to me were my saviours; another fact I couldn't see at the time. How could I see it? I was blinded by the selfishness that depression brings along as its friend.

I began to deal with it in the only way I knew how - I shut myself off and cried. If I wanted a cup of tea I had no energy or inclination to get off the settee to make it. I lived on take-away food because I couldn't face the crowds in the supermarkets. I put on more weight. I liked myself less. I couldn't be bothered to sort it out - I couldn't have anyway.

That summer I was sent to the hospital for scans and tests on my kidneys. I'd suffered so many infections they had to be sure nothing was wrong. Every scan and blood test came back clear - there was nothing physically wrong with me.

Every ailment had been caused by the underlying depression and the symptoms were merely the physical body's way of saying STOP!

I did have good days, and on those days I would go out with friends or family, maybe for lunch. I'd be OK for a while, and then, why my mind turned the taps on again I'll never know. One minute I was chatting away, the next… tears in my lunch.

My past appeared to come back to haunt me. People and situations that had previously caused me pain hurt me all over again. Why was this happening to me? I'd got over life's hurts so why now did they appear before me like huge mountains waiting for me to climb? I couldn't climb them. I no longer had the tools required: strength, positivity, insight and forgiveness. I felt hate and anger at those from my past and blamed them for how I was feeling.

The days that were the hardest were those when I was told, 'Snap out of it.' 'Pull yourself together.' 'Everybody has bad days.' 'What's wrong with you?' 'Don't be silly.' 'Things will be better tomorrow, it'll pass.' Anyone who has suffered or is suffering from depression will be familiar with these sayings from those who care about us.

A message to all those who care: Please do not say any of the above. They make it WORSE!

Following my doctor's advice, I came to the conclusion that I had to spend some time with a counsellor; somebody who would listen and not judge; somebody who would just hand me tissues when I cried.

As I sat on the edge of my bed with my hand wavering over the handset I knew that, as difficult as this call would be, I had to believe that there was someone out there who could hold my hand throughout this part of my journey. I looked at the number on the card in front of me, took a deep breath, dialled the code, cried and hung up. I did this a number of times before finally dialling the full number.

I waited for the phone to be answered, almost counting the ring tones. I silently begged them to answer because if it rang for too long I knew that my courage would leave me and I would hang up again. After what seemed like a lifetime the phone was answered and I tentatively stood on another stepping stone towards my recovery.

As I explained through the tears how I felt, the person on the other end of the phone listened. The understanding and compassion in their voice as they explained that they would get a counsellor to call me so I could make an appointment to see them was such a relief. That phone call was probably the hardest call I've ever had to make but now I realise that without making it I would've been stuck in the vicious circle I'd got caught up in.

With my first counselling session in the diary I felt a little lighter and I counted the days until my first appointment. Unfortunately this was not an overnight cure but throughout the following months, as I spent more time in counselling, I found myself waking up to a few truths about how I had driven myself to the depths of the depression that had enveloped me.

My counsellor guided me through a journey of past hurts and showed me how, even though I thought I'd done well in clearing my way through the brambles, I hadn't done the thorough job I thought I had. I got through many glasses of water, cups of tea and tissues. He was a stranger and yet I managed to pour out all my inner hurts, past and present. My fears for the future were understood and dealt with by me. He simply helped because he listened to me, he wasn't judgemental and he understood the pain.

One thing I'm so grateful to my counsellor for was this advice: 'Before you go to bed at night, always have a plan for the next day.' At the time I thought, *Oh, OK then.* It seemed like a small piece of advice; however, it came to play a huge part in my recovery. I discovered that if I planned the day ahead the night before, it gave me something to get up for. I would plan something for the next morning every night. Now sometimes this was easier than others as I didn't always feel like planning anything, but I have to admit it became easier to achieve over time and truly helped me to move forward.

I would always leave my counselling sessions feeling a little lighter, a little sunnier and a lot more convinced that, with time, I could and I would beat depression. I would become the owner of my life again someday.

Then I would get home... and there they were again: tears.

Home at this point had succumbed to dry rot, an issue I could well have done without. I cried about that too. At least I felt I had a valid reason to shed some tears then.

This was not an easy time in my life. The dark tunnel of despair seemed to get deeper and denser daily. If I was asked whether I contemplated suicide, as much as it hurts to admit it as I'm sure it will hurt those that knew then and will know now, yes I did. It seemed like the only route out. I didn't want to feel the pain in my mind anymore and I didn't want to hurt those around me with my continuing depression.

To this day I thank God for the people in my life who were there for me at these lowest points: they know who they are.

I never went as far as trying to end my life. My deepest love for those closest to me stopped me, however much I was hurting. Thoughts would strike me like lightning and make me wake up to how much pain my actions would cause others.

It was at a low point such as this, when I upset someone very close to me, that I realised I had to take the next step to recovery: anti-depressants.

Through the shadow of the darkness there is a light - be strong and press the switch

The Next Step

I don't need tablets
Give them a go
NO
I don't want to be addicted
You won't
NO
They won't help me
How do you know?
NO
I can't do this anymore
Well try the tablets
MAYBE
Are they addictive?
Let's talk about it
OK
Will they help?
Shall we try?
MAYBE
Do I need them?
You must decide that
YES

Chapter 3

I clearly remember the day I made the decision to listen to medical advice and take a course of anti-depressants: I'd woken up with a pain in my heart because I'd hurt someone so very close to me. I picked up the phone the minute the surgery opened and with trepidation made the call.

I requested an emergency appointment and was at the doctor's an hour later.

There, the next step of my journey took place. I was afraid. I didn't want to become addicted but I didn't want to be in the darkest of dark places anymore either.

I didn't want to feel tired, sad and angry. I wanted the tears to stop. I wanted to feel alive and happy again. I needed to regain my soul and bring back its positivity. If taking anti-depressants was going to help then that had to happen, that had to be the next stepping stone.

I sat there as the doctor explained everything: what effect the tablets would have, any side effects that may happen, how they would work and, most importantly of all, how they would help.

I left the surgery and felt relief that, if what the doctor had told me were true, I would soon be in a stronger position to turn my life around. I'd been informed that it could take up to three months for the tablets to take effect.

I was still seeing my counsellor at this point so at our next meeting I talked about my decision to take the medication. I received support and understanding from him as he re-iterated what my doctor had told me. We talked through how I felt about the anti-depressants and how, ultimately, I was in control. I just needed to relax and let them work for me.

At that point I made a conscious effort to wake up to what I had to do to help this happen. I realised that I had all the medical support I needed; a counsellor who listened and understood, along with family and friends who wanted one thing - for me to recover. I had to do it for them, but ultimately for me.

There was no immediate effect. I didn't suddenly start singing from the rooftops but, on the plus side, I didn't walk around in a bleak daze. I'll confess that I suffered many setbacks: I had to deal with the apartment and its dry rot; relationships were buckling under the strain of my illness. Even with medication I still suffered panic attacks at the thought of returning to work and everyday life as others knew it.

I was struggling. The counselling was still helping but I knew that perseverance with the medication, along with the counselling, was the way forward.

I couldn't commute anywhere unless by car as crowds petrified me. My partner at the time did manage to get me on a plane to Dublin but I was suffering terrible paranoia; why was that waitress in the café in Dublin talking about me? My trust in others had been completely shot. I would question everybody's motives: *Why? What? When? How?* Analysing everyone and all situations became completely normal behaviour for me.

This is the point I was at three months into being diagnosed with anxiety and depression. The previous two years had taken their toll. I was tired but I had to start to question my future. I wanted to return to work but my health was such that I couldn't cope with the structured nature of it. People outside my close family or friends were strangers wearing the darkest cloaks.

I was and am a people person, so to feel like that was so unsettling. I'd always enjoyed meeting new people and looked forward to socializing at events. At this point these situations all seemed like a lifetime away. I'd cry and scream, 'I want my life back – *PLEASE!*'

I'd spend hours wondering whether this was it for life. Was I ever going to be able to feel the sunshine inside again? No one could answer my questions and I, for sure, didn't know.

During the autumn of 2009 I had to move out of my

apartment; just something else to add to the mix! My home had become uninhabitable due to the dry rot. Going through the floor in the bedroom as the rot spread throughout my home was the last straw, so more sadness spread throughout my mind.

It was at this time that I moved in with my partner. I was grateful that at least I had a roof over my head. As the builders moved in, the heart of my home was ripped out. I'd ask myself, *Could things possibly get worse?*

It seemed like I had a continuous fight on my hands as things collapsed around me. Again and again I'd wonder how I was going to get through this. It was then I would find support in the medical team and those closest to me.

As I approached Christmas 2009, I had to admit to myself and others that returning to work was not an option in the near future. This resulted in me having to leave my employment in the corporate world. After thirty years in senior management roles I felt sad and I had no idea what the future held.

The dry rot problem at my property had been sorted out but moving back home was still not possible. I now had to get workmen in to rectify the plumbing, the electrics and the plastering. There were a few months work ahead yet. Still, I wasn't homeless, which was a major positive in the grand scheme of things.

It was at this time, while sorting through some boxes in the basement area of my apartment, that I was drawn to a number of books explaining positive thinking and its power.

Could these books hold the key to the door of recovery?

Among these books was *Love Life, Live Life* by Sue Stone. I'd purchased this book in 2008, the year before my burnout had taken hold. As I flicked through the dusty pages certain words caught my eye: affirmations, gratitude lists, visualisation, the power of your thoughts creating your reality. What if this was true? Could I incorporate the skills and tips in these books to assist me in turning my life around?

There was only one way to find out. I'd tried counselling and was now on medication so maybe they could provide some of the final answers. To me they could do no harm, only help in my recovery.

As I thought about the words in front of me I started to realise that over the last few weeks my mood had started to lift. I felt like the medication and counselling had, in their way, strengthened my belief that in time I could finally recover and the black cloud would lift to reveal sunshine again.

My trust in people was still severed, my paranoia still not good - why the lady in the shop had it in for me when I took back a faulty iron I will never know! The tears still fell, just not as often which felt good. I would still get panic attacks in crowds, commuting was still not an option but hey, somewhere out there I could see the smallest shaft of sunlight.

On finding the books I felt I'd been given a gift. If I could concentrate on devoting some time to reading them, I believed I could start the next stage of my journey.

It was that belief that helped me turn a corner because I realised, that to have that belief, I had to have felt it deep inside. My self-belief was returning. Wow, what a feeling!

Then...

Christmas 2009 brought with it my last challenge of the year. Christmas with my partner in our home had all been planned, however that wasn't quite meant to be. It was at that precise time he left me! Two days before Christmas saw me alone. Standing on my own in the snow in my slippers was how I remember it. Of course I cried again. This surely was the last straw. What else could be thrown at me?

It's sufficient to say now, in hindsight, that what felt at the time like the final straw, turned out to be the most amazing gift.

From this I was given the strength and courage to stand tall. I knew that if I passed this greatest test then recovery would be the reward.

I spent Christmas with my loving family. It snowed a lot in December 2009, but when it thawed it left the path ahead glistening with rainbow light, and that's how I felt about my life.

As 2009, my annus horribilis, drew to a close, I decided that I had two options. I could stay as I had been, and allow depression to envelop my soul every day, or I could take the risk of making my life happen - to make dramatic changes, to take risks and start getting others to believe in me again, by firstly believing in myself.

New Years Eve 2009 helped me turn a corner.

I spent it with some very dear supportive friends who that night helped me smile through the pain. I drank champagne with them and suddenly realised I could taste again.

I tasted my future and all that I knew it could bring. That night I made the conscious decision that if I was going to beat depression I should no longer let it beat me. I knew I had a fight on my hands, but I was determined to win.

Depression may have won the battle, but I was going to win the war.

I toasted the start of 2010 with laughter (that was a novelty) and tears. I had a plan.

I would renovate my property and put it on the market; I would continue with the medication until I no longer needed it; I would read as much about positive thinking, visualisation and the law of attraction as I could, then through this I would study to become a life coach in order to inspire others. I would stand tall and shout, 'I did it. I won. Look at me!'

That night, for the first time in a long time, I fell asleep smiling.

Never be afraid to take the options laid out before you

Happy New Year

Today is a New Day
A New Year
My soul will Awaken
To each new day
Enlightened
Happy
Spirited to live life
To the full
The rest of my life
Starts here...

Chapter 4

As I awoke on New Year's Day 2010, I realised that although I was surrounded by lots of love and support from family and friends, I was alone with my decisions and where my journey would take me.

I took that day to sit and contemplate my future and all that it held. The snow was still on the ground outside, but I now felt warmth surrounding my soul. I decided that I was never ever going back down the road I'd travelled. Somehow, someway, I was going to change my world and, through that, inspire and motivate others to do the same.

Following the inevitable decision to leave my employment in November 2009, I realised that I now wanted to work for myself. I took some quiet time out and thought about what it was I wanted to do with my life. On taking the time to read *Love Life, Live Life* and listen to Sue Stone's CD again, I realised that that was what I wanted to do. I wanted to work on transforming my life and study for a life-coaching diploma. I realised that by studying for this I could put it into practice as a business to help others.

This was it, my light bulb moment. I would get better, I would study and I would transform my life. Eureka!

At this point I put out a very clear message to the Universe and all who would listen. I'd been inspired and one day I would meet with Sue Stone to thank her. I would, like Sue, inspire and motivate others.

Now doesn't that seem easy? Sounds great, but...

As anyone who's been faced with depression knows, words are easy. It's the actual doing that takes a little time. I knew that while I was capable of doing all I wanted to do, I first of all had to overcome a good many obstacles.

The first was renovating my apartment. Since I'd been left alone at Christmas, I now had nowhere to live. In trepidation I set about planning how I was going to achieve the re-decoration of a 1400 square-foot apartment. The one lesson I'd learnt was to take each day one step at a time; I knew it was the only way forward. The next item on the agenda was to undertake the course to obtain my diploma.

By January 2nd 2010, I'd set out a path ahead on paper. I knew from reading all the books that if I wrote it down, believed and visualised my path, I could and would achieve all my goals. Determination had to become my middle name again.

The goals I set myself were:

I would paint every one of the ten rooms in the apartment (yes it was larger than the average house) by the end of March 2010.

I would complete my life coaching course by the end of June 2010 (I had 12 months to do it in but this was me on a mission).

I would not have a TV in the apartment I was decorating; I didn't want or need distractions.

I would set up my own business by the end of July 2010.

My friends and family looked at me aghast: was I mad? How could I possibly do all of the above in the time limits I'd set myself? At the time I wondered too, but I understood that if I didn't believe in myself and my goals then I couldn't expect others to either.

The determination I gathered from inside me was incredible. I continued to read a number of books which motivated me and re-assured me that if I stayed positive it would become a habit and I would achieve what I'd set out to do.

I was so determined that, as 2009 had truly been the worst year of my life, there was no way I could ever allow myself to travel backwards towards it. I had it set in my mind that, as bad as 2009 had been, 2010 was going to be the exact opposite. I would reach the end of it much happier, a lot calmer and more positive.

My first stepping stone was to come to terms with the realisation that I no longer had someone close to share my aspirations with. I had plenty of family and friends but no partner to share the good or the bad times. This realisation shook me, but it did make me realise that if I could get through this and out the other side, then I could do anything.

Having not had the confidence to go to the local superstore on my own in 2009, I found myself realising that this was the first step. Alas, if I didn't go then I would have no food and no decorating materials to carry out the major task I now had in hand.

With this in mind, on January 3rd I set off on a shaky journey to do my shopping. That's when I sat there on a bench and cried for all the memories associated with shopping at my local store. Last time I hadn't been alone. How was I going to do this: face people?

I looked around and realised that the only person stopping me from grabbing that trolley was me. With nervousness I held onto to the trolley as if it was a lifeline and, as I pushed that trolley around, I thought about my apartment, how it was going to look when I'd finished it, how proud I would feel when I'd achieved my goal. I practised ridding my mind of negative thoughts and replacing them with positive ones. Again I rejoiced in the sense of my achievement. I smiled at the lady at the cash desk; she smiled back. I then got back into the car and cried with exhaustion!

I cried as I unloaded my car and I cried when I visited my neighbour who re-assured me it was normal to feel the way I did. I was allowed to let it all out if that's what I wanted to do. I was given a hug and, thankfully, NOT told it would all be OK.

I was so fortunate to have people around me who understood how I felt, who didn't rush me through the get-better-soon process, who allowed me to be me.

It was because of them that I held onto the power inside, the power of my intuition - an intuition that allowed me to tell myself it would all be OK.

Throughout January 2010 I had many days of feeling like this, but every time it happened I would allow myself some time to cry and to feel sorry for myself, then I would always follow it with a soul searching conversation of, 'What next?' I spent my days painting anything that stood still in the apartment. I would chat to the workmen who were helping me out and at times I would actually find myself laughing at some of their jokes. Now smiling was a new thing - but it worked!

I was a person who was normally content with silence, but this was not the time. I had the radio on constantly; the music helped me to switch off any negative thoughts of the past. The radio 2 presenters became my virtual friends, I would join in with the discussions as I painted, they couldn't hear me but I voiced my opinion anyway! I couldn't allow any other distractions if I was to reach my targets.

I had friends ask, 'What if you haven't finished the decorating by the end of March?' I would answer, 'There is no what if?' It sounded mad, but I now recognise it as the start of my using the power of thought without being conscious of it.

It's a true saying - mind over matter.

I painted and painted and painted. I painted in 2010 as much as I'd cried in 2009. I had fun and the satisfaction of looking back at what I'd achieved at the end of each day was amazing. I'd send photos to friends and I'd smile to myself with pride. This, in my eyes, was my therapy.

I was giving my life a makeover. With no TV in the apartment I had no negative news to watch or listen to; I only had music and books. This truly was a transformational time. It re-focused my mind in a way that I never thought possible. Counselling and medication had helped but not in the way this had. The power of the sense of achievement. Nothing ever matches it.

Each day is a stepping stone on your life journey

Take some time out today to write down some goals. There is no need to rush this process, do it in your own time. Set small goals and a couple of challenging ones for the longer term.

Another Reason To Cry

To know you had moved on
Hit hard
Life is a series of experiences
That will bring you a lesson
Just search for the light
That
Brightens your path
It is always ahead of you!

Chapter 5

My mission to decorate my apartment was well underway and you may wonder how I survived when I laid down my paintbrush for the day, in the evening in an apartment with no television. Well, I studied. I had to complete seven assignments in order to obtain my diploma and as I wanted to do this by June 2010, I had to get on with it.

I spent my evenings studying, researching and typing up my assignments. I can't even begin to explain how I felt when in January 2010 my first contribution came back marked with an 'A'. I was never a natural student and although I've passed many examinations, I've had very few 'A' grades. So you can imagine what this did for my confidence.

With great excitement I rang my parents and told them the news. After all I'd been through, they were thrilled. I'm not ashamed to say this time I cried with happiness and sheer joy. It had been a very long time since I'd enjoyed that feeling. And then...

Another shock made me cry all over again, with sadness.

It was at this time I discovered that the person I still cared about so much, even though he'd left, had moved on with someone else and therefore completely out of my life. All my memories were so raw, I felt like my scars had again been opened up and my heart had been torn apart. I entered another difficult time. Just as I felt I was on the road to becoming a stronger, more confident person, I was hit with this realisation. Sadness again enveloped me.

I felt that, along with the depression, I was now carrying around a heavy heart. What on earth was the answer to this one? I sat in the middle of my decorating mess and literally felt myself crumble. 'Help me,' I cried, but at that moment nobody was there to listen. Surely I'd been through enough? Why then did I feel like

I'd been hit by a thunderbolt all over again?

I had to talk to somebody, but it had to be a stranger. I searched the internet and rang a relationship counsellor to make an appointment. I was still on the medication and, having spent some time in 2009 with a counsellor, I decided to return to some therapy. I knew if I didn't I would struggle again and this time, as I'd fought so hard to get to where I was, I couldn't allow that to happen.

Oh, how I ached. I cried again and searched for answers that weren't forthcoming. My head thumped with jumbled thoughts of sadness, but yet deep inside I felt that if I just tried to work this out I would return to the sense of well-being and positivity that had carried me through the first two months of 2010.

Noting the appointment in my diary for two days ahead, I carried out an exercise that I'd practiced many times. In my mind I took a notepad and scribbled down all my negative and sad thoughts. I then imagined scrunching them up into a ball and throwing them into a bin. I wrote a gratitude list for all the good I had in my life, and I re-read my affirmations and goals list. I then stood up, and in the knowledge that I had an appointment to talk to somebody, turned on the radio and started painting again.

The days passed and I drove to my appointment thinking, *Am I doing the right thing, I feel a bit better today?* Fifteen minutes into the appointment I was in no doubt I was in the right place as I found myself pouring my heart out and my tears into another box of tissues!

The one thing that depression has taught me is that however alone you feel, there's always someone out there to listen and help. It's down to one's self to be brave and to realise these people are readily available to hold your hand along the path of recovery. **Never be afraid to pick up that phone.**

As I talked I realised how far I'd come along my path of recovery, and if I could now just carry on with the mission statement that I'd made to myself in January, I could work this out with the help of others.

On getting home that day I stood tall and realised that all I'd had was a temporary setback. This was a first but I'd been assured it may not be the last. The knowledge of this made me take stock and return to the 'one day at a time' process I had come to know so well. After all, it isn't how many times you get knocked down, it's the amount of times you get up, stand tall and look the world ahead straight on that really counts.

I clutched at any straw that was handed to me at this time. I took opportunities to visit friends and family.When I wasn't decorating or studying I was out and about trying to build some normality into my life. I knew that if I didn't focus on the aims ahead and visualise their outcome I'd get lost again.

As I painted every wall, radiator, door and skirting board, I'd hold close all my dreams. I knew that once I'd finished the painting I had to turn my focus to my next big venture - my business!

I would talk about my business to anyone who would listen. The workmen were all great sounding boards: I would tell them how I was studying for my life coaching diploma; how I intended to go out into the world to help others live their dreams. They would ask questions and talk about their visions, their dreams. I started to realise that as I talked I became lighter and my soul stirred inside with the excitement of becoming self-employed as a coach, an author and a speaker.

I enjoyed my study time and the research that went into the assignments. I discovered more and more about the avenues I wanted to travel down and the people I aspired to be like. I found myself connecting with people who had a similar aspiration, which was to spread positivity around the globe. I became fasci-nated by the law of attraction and how it worked.

I kept all my learning in my mind as I continued to paint my apartment and I'm proud to say that on March 24th 2010 I laid down my paintbrush having achieved my target with the most amazing results. Not one member of my family or friends had been allowed to enter through the door until my mission was complete. Were they amazed? You can bet on it! As they all took time to visit, I was elated at their comments. I was again smiling inside and out.

'It looks like a show home. Did you really do all this yourself?' was a common comment. I stood tall and soaked it all in. I had done it. I'd achieved the first thing on my list.

I continued with my counselling sessions which helped me focus on my journey. I came to understand that it was my relationship with myself which had determined the outcome of several relationships in my life. I learnt that I was not always responsible for others' feelings and, far from constantly playing the rescuer, I now needed time out for me to rescue myself. I needed to allow others to help me when I needed it, to ask for help and to be honest with myself. I didn't need to always be the strong one; it was OK to walk away. But when the time required it, it was OK to stand up and be counted.

The completion of the decorating marked a huge turning point on my journey. I'd done what I'd set out to do, and it made me realise that by having something positive to focus on your mind can be turned away from negative thoughts and feelings.

Even though the first three months of 2010 had provided me with a couple of stumbling blocks, I'd woken up to many good things too. One of these was the writing of my gratitude list on a daily basis, always finding something new to add.

This is something I found to be a constant positive in my life. When I took time out to be grateful for all the things I had, instead of the things I didn't have, it lifted my spirit, it made me smile and allowed my thoughts to be conscious of the now, along with my future, lightened by all the good it had in store.

If you haven't got a gratitude list take some time out to write one. Keep it close to you, read it at bedtime and again when you wake up. Each one of us has things to be grateful for, however small or big. Allow this list to help you and lift your spirits whenever needed.

Live for the now, be grateful and smile. Smiling suits you!

Take time out to write a list of all the things you are grateful for in your life – however big or small, they are all of equal importance

A New Dawn

I have turned a corner
Only I can see
I smile inside as
The warmth of its direction
Curls itself around
My heart
As
My thoughts
Turn to light the
Way ahead.

Chapter 6

I'd decided that as I had now decorated my apartment it was time to put it on the market. It was with mixed feelings that I invited estate agents around to value it. So much of me wanted to rid myself of the place where the anguish had started and where I had suffered so much negativity, yet it held so many memories good and bad. I just felt it had to go.

The mixed feelings came as I realised how much work I'd done to transform it to a newer, brighter home. It was now an apartment with a completely renovated basement which I could use as an office. Its gutted bathroom had been replaced with a fully tiled show bathroom and I loved it. Still, I had to let it go, didn't I?

I had an inner voice telling me, *Live here a while. Leave it when it's a home, not now when you view it as a refuge from the outside world.* So I invited people in to visit, to share dinner, and every month that went by with no potential buyers was another month in which to build a home within the four walls that had seen so much sadness.

During the months of March 2010 to August 2010 I underwent a massive shift in my thinking. The completion of the decorating was proof that if I set a target and visualised it, then I could make it happen.

As I spent my evenings studying - still without a TV – I'd concentrate very hard on the grade I wanted to achieve in my assignments. I felt disappointment when my second assignment was returned with a 'B' grade. I thought back to the books I'd read and realised that as the initial assignment was graded 'A' I'd encountered a sense of disbelief. It was this disbelief that had resulted in the 'B' grade: I'd brought it on myself and turned it into reality through my thoughts.

Following this event I decided that I'd really test this law of attraction theory. To do this I'd write an 'A' on the completed work I kept as a copy and visualise the tutor marking the same on his copy. I almost felt like it was a game, a test of my ability and the 'law'. Guess who won?

Yep, the 'law'. Out of my seven submitted assignments I only ever had that one 'B'. The other six were all marked with a big bold 'A', just as I'd visualised. Powerful eh? I realised at this time that if you're willing to put the work and effort in, then the Universe will do what it can to provide you with the assistance you need to attain the results you desire.

It was in my target month of June 2010 when I received notification of my achievement:

A life-coaching diploma with a distinction!

I was so happy, and it felt that finally I was heading towards claiming back my good health.

Two of the targets I'd set myself in January had now come to fruition. The months had not always been easy; while I'd recaptured the art of visualisation I'd come to realise a lot of things.

I came to understand that while you may set the intention of your desire or aspiration out there to the Universe in thoughts, it's given strength by writing it down and understanding the feeling of what it's like to be living it.

In January 2010 I'd sat down with my notebook and done just that. I'd read the books and understood how this 'stuff' was supposed to work. I'd seen my renovated apartment in my mind's eye, I'd imagined my diploma success - and here I was in June 2010, living it!

I know it didn't come alone, there was hard work involved from me but, because I had set the intention, the number of people and situations that crossed my path just at the right time was phenomenal. It was this that helped and guided me forward.

I learnt the art of determination and that if I wanted or

needed something badly enough, I would receive it. I learnt a huge lesson of clarity (this I'll share with you in the next chapter) and boy is clarity important!

I still had days where things seemed to hurt, but because of the medical help and counselling I was receiving, I truly was now crying less.

The biggest obstacle I had to overcome was my fear of public transport. Panic attacks would engulf me at the thought of a journey by any means other than the safety of my own car. I tried to do it, really I did, but a panic attack would hold me back every time.

The experience of not being able to get my breath, the exhausting pull of air from my lungs which caused a stitch-like pain in my chest, is something that I'll never forget. I was told that in time this would ease and I'd be able to face my fear and paranoia. I truly hoped it would.

I guess the question is, if I could use the visualisation method to reach physical goals, why couldn't I use it to overcome this fear? At the time I didn't even think it an option. I was so scared of being back where I was in 2009 that avoidance of any situation that may bring on an attack was far easier than dealing with it head on.

It felt quite bizarre to have achieved so much in 2010, yet this one mountain just seemed too difficult to climb. I decided that in time I'd find a way and that in the meantime I'd set about completing my next vision:

My business.

Always believe you can

Take time out to write here one action you will take within the next 24 hours that will take you towards one of your goals.

Starting Again

The time is now
To start work
To re-enter the world
Of employment
Weird, strange
Yet so satisfying that
Now I work
For ME!

Chapter 7

As I explained in Chapter 6, your visions truly have to be clear and focussed.

It was while I was planning my business, contemplating how I was going to work with people, what it would be called and where to start, that a realisation came to me about how powerful words and visualisations truly are.

Clarity

As I've explained, when I suffered burnout I'd been working in senior management roles for 30 years. Corporate life was a way of life, but I'd become tired. To this day I remember sitting in my office suffering a panic attack with no one around to help, crying, 'I just want out of this, I can't do this anymore.' Was burnout the Universe's answer?

Also at this time the bathroom at the apartment had been damaged by a leak from the apartment above. I'd look around it and think *I hate this bathroom, it's such a mess. I want a new modern bathroom.* Was a radiator leak which led to dry rot the Universe's answer?

As I took time to look back on these two events it came to me that while I'd requested a way out and a new bathroom, I hadn't exactly been clear in what I'd asked for. The answers to my requests had most certainly arrived, but by no means in the form that I'd wished. Lessons most certainly learnt!

I realised that I if I was now going to take coaching out into the world I'd have to be very clear from the outset as to what my plans and objectives were.

I felt that while I was now in possession of my life coaching diploma, I had so much more to give. I wanted to start a business that could help anyone realise their dreams. I woke up and recognised that despite the diploma, it was my life experiences and my determination to always win through that would inspire and help others. From my heart I would declare, 'I am not a text book coach,' therefore it would be my aim to utilise all my skills learnt from life and my career to, 'Light your journey ahead.'

With my house still on the market I knew that time, along with money, would soon run out and that I'd need to get help from whatever avenues I could in order to build a business that was going to earn me a living. This, I can tell you now, was much easier said than done.

I decided I needed a name, a brand. Having been in the corporate world for all those years I understood the need for an identity - a business identity.

I was fortunate that as I was struggling to decide the answer to this question I was visiting friends, who suggested, 'Awaken.' 'Fantastic!' was my response; it said it all. After all I'd come through a period of awakening myself, and this was exactly what I wanted others to do with my help.

The colours of my brand were easy. wanted calm, relaxed and approachable navy with the gorgeous sunflower yellow, standing tall and offering its message of confidence and courage.

I was on the next leg of my journey. I was so scared. It had been scarcely a year since I'd hidden under my duvet, crying into my pillow, and here I was in a newly renovated property, armed with a new qualification and about to stand on the first stepping stone of self-employment.

As strong as I appeared to other people, it was not always what I felt inside. I was still on the medication and attending my counselling sessions, but as I discussed my plans with my doctor and counsellor I was encouraged that I could do exactly what I'd planned. I could become self-employed as a coach, I had the ability through my experiences to understand what others were going through and they assured me that, because of the journey I'd been on, I was in a strong place to inspire others to move their lives forward.

I started to take stock of all my life experiences to date. I could use all the situations I'd been through, including all of those in the last year, to inspire and motivate people. I could help them see that my life was an abundance of experiences - I had walked in many shoes and here was my opportunity to share this with them and prove that there is always light.

I now had to put all my words into practice. It was all very good telling family, friends and anyone who would listen I was about to start a business and go self employed. Now was the time to do it.

I sought out business assistance from local free agencies, scoured the internet for guidance and spoke to business owners who at one time had all been in the shoes of the newly self-employed. All this help proved to be invaluable and again proved the point, you are never alone.

Following many discussions I now had a business plan and a website in progress. I set off down the road, smiling as I stepped onto the next stepping stone of my journey.

Awaken had woken up!

**Always keep your destination at the forefront of your mind
Ensure you enjoy the journey on the way**

Take time out today to look back at your goal list. Have you achieved any of them? If so congratulate yourself and celebrate! Do all your plans have clarity? If not re-write them, take time to work through what it is you really desire.

Smile in Colour

It's now time to smile,
Smile more than I cry
Sunshine is back
And
The cold lonely
Days of sadness
Are being replaced
By the true colour
Of the rainbow
Ahead

Chapter 8

'Awaken'. Every day the name resonates with me more than the day before. July 2010 saw me tiptoeing around a start date. It was going to be June 2010, then July 2010, and then I pulled myself up, took some time out and questioned my delaying tactics.

Why was I so afraid? I'd done so much in the last 52 weeks; surely it would be OK, wouldn't it?

It was at this time I returned to a number of the self-help books that I'd collected over time. I began to work again at the power of the law of attraction. I began to scribble down notes at every given opportunity about my business and what it was going to achieve.

I thought about what I'd come through. I'd been through so many tears, but then I realised that if I started to focus on the feelings of being scared and the sadness, my thoughts could become reality again and I would indeed go backwards. I also knew that the only way forward was to work on, and in, my own company. Going back to a corporate role would feel like entering a world I no longer belonged in.

No! All of this negativity had to stop, NOW.

This had to be turned round into a positive. I carried out the tried and tested scenario in my mind, and slowly but surely it turned like a wheel. I turned the key to start the engine, and as I accelerated all my energy into the positive thoughts, so they gathered speed and momentum.

I found myself lying awake with the excitement of being self-employed. I wrote another gratitude list of all the opportunities that had presented themselves to me over the last year for which I was now eternally grateful.

Affirmations

These I'd learnt about in the books I'd read. I now felt confident enough to write my own list of affirmations.

I'd learnt that affirmations are words or sentences which you write down, believe in and feel everyday. They inspire you to live the life you imagine. My affirmations included:

I am confident and I now have my own business, Awaken Life Coaching.

I have a successful business that inspires and motivates others.

I am healthy and will continue to work on improving my well-being.

I will sell my property when the time is right.

I have met a large number of new contacts and I am continually spreading my message.

Along with my gratitude list, these affirmations gave me clarity on where the path of my journey would take me next.

I learnt that once affirmations are written you have to read them often and truly believe you are living them then and there. As I did this, the reality of my business started to take shape.

I started to research more and more on the internet, talked to others in business and then was invited to a network event. It was here I realised that a lot of new business owners felt the same as I did. I wasn't feeling scared because I'd been depressed - it was a natural feeling for anyone setting out into the unknown.

What a revelation! I also spoke to a good many people over this time that had indeed suffered themselves from similar burnout situations. *Maybe somebody should tell the corporate world,* I thought.

By August 2nd 2010 I was ready, and I made the call to tell HMRC I was now in business.

This was followed by texts to everyone on my mobile, posts on social media and phone calls to everyone else I knew. I wanted to shout my news from the roof tops. I was excited, happy and very proud to be a business owner. Having said that, it was a couple of weeks before it hit me.

There I was sitting at the traffic lights when out of nowhere came, *Oh my goodness I own a business - all by myself – amazing!*

Do not let fear hold you back – grab it and shake it off like an old wet overcoat!

Take time out to write your affirmations list.

Remember affirmations always start with positive real time wording.

I am, I can, I will, I have, I do..... etc

Feel what is like to live the affirmation, be determined and believe.

I'm On My Way

Any new beginning is
A daunting thought
Any new day
Can bring the unexpected
Any new idea
Has the potential
To become huge
Hold on to
Your dream…

Chapter 9

With the decision taken and the phone call made you'd think I was ready to start on the journey ahead. I felt afraid, but not once did I ever think I'd made a crazy decision.

I knew that whatever happened I would make this work. I had a desire to be a success and to share my story with all who would listen. Through my journey I wanted to inspire others to live the life they desired and to live their dreams.

At the time I was asked, 'How will people know who you are?' I didn't have a clue; I would just have to work it out somehow!

I truly believed that if I could put into practice all my research, continue to work on the process of eliminating negative thought patterns and give my dreams clarity along with determination, I could achieve exactly what I wanted: a successful business along with the sale of my apartment which would lead to money in the bank.

I'd sit every day and visualise my future. I knew that thinking too much about my past and the path it had taken me on would only lead to further periods of darkness and depression. I painted my days with bright colours in my mind and spent as much time with others as I could, telling them all I'd learnt.

I'm not about to tell you that it was easy. There were days when I'd be taken back to my past by an event, or something as simple as a song on the radio would set my thoughts into a backward spiral. However, what I can tell you is that the best thing to do is to go with that - follow the skid, don't try and steer yourself out of it quickly. I'd have what I called 'wobble days', which is a phrase I adopted from Sue Stone of *Love Life, Live Life*.

Wobble days could occur when I least expected them. I'd be so happy one day, and the next the quietness of the phone and the loudness of the bank statement falling through the letterbox onto the mat could bring one on. There were also days when nothing had changed but I'd wake up in a melancholy mood with absolutely no idea why. It was on these days I'd once more think, *It's not fair. Why can't I be positively happy ALL of the time?*

I came to accept and understand that in the beginning, going with the flow of these days was the best option, fighting against them was useless. I'd take time out to think about my future, re-read my self-help books, do some more research or call family or friends who understood and listened without handing out well-meaning advice.

I found that the more I could concentrate my thoughts on my future, with all its positivity and abundance of happiness, the less anxious I'd become. I realised after a while that if I had a wobble day, I had to have a plan.

I made the decision that if I woke up and a mist had formed I'd start the day with a blast of music. Uplifting, soul-energising music. Dancing around the living room I found was a great way to get rid of the cobwebs. I'd consciously say to myself that I'd be showered and dressed within an hour of getting out of bed - that way lounging around in my dressing gown was not an option.

It was on the days I had no plan in my diary that I'd wobble the most. It was then I'd action a visit to family or friends, read a good book or work on my business. But whatever it was, I made sure it would occupy my mind fully.

As a wobble day drew to a close I'd go to bed feeling that, even though I'd started a little low, I'd finished at least on the first or second rung of the ladder. I always fell asleep on these days believing the next day would be better, and they almost always were. It was at the end of wobble days when I'd revert back to my counsellor's advice of, 'Always have a plan for the next day.' This ensured that the next day started on a positive note and wobbles could be banished before they began.

I'm pleased to say that with a business to run my wobble days became fewer and fewer, with bigger gaps in between. I was meeting so many new people and started to believe that enjoyment in all areas of my life was now attainable.

As the months went past with no viewings of the apartment I began to wonder what my next steps were. I had equity in my property, but when I needed cash there was little point in it being tied up in bricks and mortar. In all honesty this was a scary period in my life. I had no confirmed regular monthly income, my savings were not as they were and I'd just started a business. I knew that, long term, this was unsustainable. I'd talk to others in business who assured me this was normal for the first year and things would change with time.

I decided that the only way was to charge ahead with my plans, to seek avenues where I could expand my knowledge and take this knowledge out to help others.

I knew deep within my heart two things:

There was no going back to the depressed state I'd felt the previous year and I would, with clarity, determination and vision, make Awaken work

I would inspire others and motivate them to 'make their life happen.'

With my gratitude and affirmations list always close to hand, I'd arm myself with total belief, walk tall, stare straight ahead and work hard to ensure that I achieved the goals I'd set myself.

Allow the stars at night to light up your dreams and plans for the days ahead

Take time out today to think about and write down your biggest challenge, set a completion date for it so you can work towards it.

I'm Back

Always believe in you
For there is no better
Person
You are the only one
Who hears the voice
Within
Smile and allow
Your soul
To always sing
Out loud
For the world to hear

Chapter 10

By Christmas 2010, I'm so proud to say, I'd achieved the following goals:

I'd painted every one of the ten rooms in the apartment by the end of March.

I'd completed my life coaching course by the end of June - with a distinction.

I still had no TV in the apartment to cause distractions.

I'd set up my own business by the end of July.

I can't even begin to tell you here what these achievements meant to me. To say I wanted to shout them all from the highest roof tops is an understatement.

Through each day of 2010 I'd worked diligently on my projects in hand. I'd worked on myself, I'd taken risks and I'd spent as much time with as many positive people as I could. I felt like I'd walked a dozen marathons.

It's true to say though, that one of my biggest challenges in 2010 faced me in the December. As I stood proud of all the achievements I'd conquered, one more daunting trial was lurking in the shadows.

I'd agreed to attend a Christmas party in a nearby city and as the snow fell on the approach to the party date I could feel the panic again start to take hold. What if the snow was so bad I couldn't drive to the party: I'd have to take public transport!

Well, as in 2009, it snowed and it snowed. The morning of the party arrived and as I stared outside I knew the roads were a no-go. I'd arranged to do a radio interview in the morning, which in hindsight was lucky. This was to be my first radio interview and as a result the nerves were wrestling with my insides which left no room for panic.

As the radio interview drew to a close I realised I had an hour in which to get changed, get to the station and face my biggest fear. In party dress and purple wellington boots I headed out through the door. I was fortunate that my neighbour had a 4x4 so I could at least get to the dreaded means of transport. 'Was this a good thing?' I asked myself.

Again, I count myself lucky that as my neighbours had been aware of my year off work, they offered to wait for me at the entrance to the train station so that if I had a panic attack they would be there to take me home. This gave me the strength to walk through the doors and, I'm so proud to say, onto the dreaded public transport.

It was amazing! As I settled into my seat, I texted family and friends with my news. It was like winning first prize. I'd done it, I'd faced my fear. The party was a success and the paranoia had abated. I had so many people to thank for their guidance, support and help. I was on my way to 2011.

But...

There was still a way to go!

I knew that even though I'd achieved my goals for 2010, I had to set many more for 2011. I had a decision to make about the apartment, which still hadn't sold. I had to find ways to expand what I was doing with the business in order that it would become profitable. I had to get my message out to more people. I had to remain positive and sustain the good health I was now enjoying.

I was still on medication for the depression but I aimed to come off it in 2011 and utilise my inner positivity to support my outer self. I'd take the learning from my research and my work to build on all I'd achieved in order to lift myself to full health and well-being.

I'll always count myself fortunate that I received the best medical help and advice I could have had. I knew that with that support my aim would be achievable. Every aspect of coming off the medication was explained in depth, just as it had been when I'd made the decision to take it. I'm so grateful that it was as a result of this that I held in my mind the knowledge that this journey would be eased by the understanding and support I always had to hand.

With the apartment not sold I took a huge step in removing it from the market. I then set about making the basement into an office. I decided that if I was serious about taking Awaken to the next level I had to get it away from the kitchen table and into a proper working environment.

I purchased office furniture and from January 2011 it became a place to work on the business. I wrote plans, came up with ideas and focussed all my energy on building a successful business.

In the first month of 2011 I was very fortunate to attend a vision board workshop. I had an amazing time with Jayne Morris, 'The Power Coach,' who helped me literally move my thinking to yet another level. Having read a lot about vision boards, I'd never made one of my own. Here, at this workshop, I was taken down another avenue on my journey and literally thanks to Jayne, walked away with my future in my hands.

I found that by placing all the things I desired in my future, along with my affirmations, on a vision board, I had something daily to focus on. This enabled me to realise these visions in my mind - to give them feeling and emotion, to live them prior to realising them. Truly amazing.

As I came away from the weekend I realised that this was something powerful I could share with others to inspire them to work on their future. I was literally in awe of how, over the following months, things I'd placed on my board were coming to life - so much so that I found myself creating another board for my business.

My wobble days became wobble moments and I found that by

focusing on my boards, and therefore my future, even my wobble moments became fewer.

As 2011 went by I realised that keeping the apartment was not a long-term option because the cost of its upkeep was too high. It was hard to come to terms with, but by March I had another huge decision to make.

Return to the employment market in order to sustain a regular monthly income which would be enough to pay for the apartment. Or sell it and move on.

This was not an easy time nor an easy decision but I felt worn down by all the attention I now had to give to keeping the apartment. I began to realise I was fed up with living a town life and longed to be back in my home village. As the money situation got tighter and cash flow became an issue I knew I had to sell.

This time I had to be clear on my visions, I had to be determined and I had to believe it would sell. I couldn't doubt in any way that a purchaser would walk through my door.

It was on a Saturday in late March 2011 that I walked through the estate agents door. I explained that I needed to sell my flat, and quickly. I stated that I needed an estate agent who was honest and positive about the sale, someone who would work to get the apartment sold ASAP. I was assured that I'd have all their support, so with that I arranged a valuation appointment.

When I arrived home that Saturday I immediately posted the estate agent's name along with my address on my vision board and wrote 'Sold by' across it.

I visualised moving out and moving back to my home village. Was it magic, fate or the law of attraction that sold my flat in 16 days?

If the power of positive thinking hadn't shown itself in many ways recently, I may well have questioned the speed of the sale. However, I'd been shown again that true belief and determination in thoughts could bring about the reality.

As I looked at my board on a daily basis, in its prime position in my office, I became in awe of the many words, pictures and situations that were now placing themselves in my life.

Moving out of my apartment, however, was a tad fraught. With move dates constantly shifting I began to despair. It was at times a struggle to keep the positive flow going, but in my heart I knew I was destined to leave the apartment, and all that went with it, behind.

I was destined for a new start, I could feel it. I knew once I'd moved I'd create the last piece of the jigsaw in my recovery. I suppose that since this was in the forefront of my mind, waiting for the inevitable seemed like an age instead of 14 weeks. Suffice to say, in all honesty, I had a few more wobble days but during this time I received the most incredible surprise which can only leave me in awe of how powerful visualisation and setting your intentions can really be.

When things seem to be moving away, stand still and wait - you will be surprised!

Take time out to carry out some further research on vision boards. Think about attending a workshop or purchase a guide and create your own board at home.

If you can visualise it, you can make it real.

Opportunities Unfolding

Never close your eyes
The possibilities that
Are in front of you
Are endless
Your mind can see them
Be still and look
Picture them
Feel them
Enjoy them
For they are on their
Way!

Chapter 11

As my move got nearer I'm pleased to say I secured a new home in the village where I grew up. The energy of my thoughts would keep me smiling as I struggled with the length of time the completion on my sale was taking.

It was tough, but it was then I realised how far I'd come along my journey to recovery. Here I was, two years on, continuing along the path and moving house with no medication and no counselling. At this time I had a conversation with a friend who commented on how well I was doing and that it was a good job I was on the medication as it was probably helping!

I have to say the look on their face was priceless when I explained that, with my doctor's support, I'd come off the medication in March 2011. I'd made a decision not to actively tell people I was off the medication to see if they would notice any difference. I felt on cloud nine at that point and so proud that I'd come so far.

Now onto the surprise.

It was as I sat in the apartment one day, surrounded by boxes, feeling very sorry for myself and wondering when the sale would complete, that an email arrived from Sue Stone.

Having signed up to Sue's database I would occasionally receive emails from her detailing her news and events, but this one was different. This one held the details of how to apply to become a Sue Stone coach and as a result become a member of the Sue Stone Foundation. Well, as they say, you could have knocked me down with a feather.

Having read Sue's book and setting the intention the previous year to meet with her and carry out similar work, here I was sat in front of my computer staring at the screen in disbelief. Was I really reading this or was I dreaming?

Being in business for a year I'd started to think of ways to spread my message further afield. I'd begun running workshops for those wanting to know more about positive thinking, I was coaching others on the creation of vision boards and I was exploring avenues to increase my learning. This was exactly the next step I wanted to take.

With great anticipation I opened up the application form and printed it out. It was completed and in the post the next day. The sheer excitement of posting that application form was tremendous, now all I had to do was to sit and wait.

Having read so many articles and books about the law of attraction and how it works I decided this was the time to test it. I thought back to the message in Sue's book and knew that if there was ever a time to test the law of attraction theory, this was it.

As I walked towards the post box I pictured in my mind my application being delivered to Sue, I thought about her opening it, reading through it and passing it onto the next stage file. As I dropped the application form into the post box I closed my eyes for a few seconds and thought about how I'd feel when I got a response and a call for interview. As you can imagine, based on the knowledge that I placed in my future two years ago in 2009 - a desire to meet and work with Sue - this thought was filled with a great excitement. I turned and walked back up to the apartment with a knowing smile in place as, in my mind, this whole sequence of events had already happened.

I then decided to take the same action with the sale of my apartment. Getting stressed about it would not speed it up but walking away would, so I moved out, leaving the boxes behind. I was very grateful to my new partner, who offered me a place to stay until the contracts were complete. I could leave you guessing, but within five days of doing this I completed on the apartment and had a move date!

The excitement of the move to my new home was now real. Again, sending positive thoughts to the outcome of my desire had worked, whereas stressing about it and holding it in a negative frame hadn't.

It was during my move that I received an email from Sue inviting me to attend an interview with her. It had happened again; I'd set my intention and the vision had become reality.

Within two weeks of sending off my application form, here I was having a telephone interview with the very lady whose book I had pulled out of a box in my dusty apartment two years earlier. As we talked, I realised that the journey I had been on during these two years was an experience through which would come a gift to inspire, help and motivate others.

Amazed is the only word that can describe how I felt when I was accepted to train with Sue in September 2011.

I moved house and soon settled back into the village life of my childhood; the secure place I now find myself, a lifetime away from the dark, dreary days of 2009. The thoughts of those days live with me, but the memories aren't so painful anymore. It would be an injustice to my experiences to erase them permanently from my mind as I believe now it all happened for a reason.

I soul-searched at that time for the reasons, but have come to realise that in life, lessons are learnt through experience and it's only when one has come out the other side that the true lesson from having to attend that experience is then shown to us.

Doesn't the magic sound too good to be true? Well true it is, and for this reason I've told you about my journey.

The final chapter of this book will take you through the lessons I've learnt on my way. If you feel lost, I hope the lessons and the story of my journey will help you to find your way.

Experience is a lesson in disguise

Take time out to review your life experiences, what have you learnt from them?

If you have a achieved any or all of your goals, CELEBRATE!

Be Thankful For The Lessons

As you look back
On every chapter
Of your life
Take time to sit
Be still
And think of
The lessons that
Were passed to you
Some at greater
Cost than others
But always an experience
To take forth and learn from

Chapter 12

This chapter reviews all my learning's along my journey. They are chronicled in order that you may see how my experience did, indeed become a great gift through the lessons it taught me.

Chapter 1

At times it's OK to be afraid. Without the fear we sometimes don't cry out for the help we so badly need.

Recognise changes in yourself. If you think you've changed you probably have – there'll be a reason why that's happened.

Seek others' opinion of you, and do not be afraid of the answer. It's through this that confirmation of your fears and their hold on you can come to light.

Admitting you need medical help is just fine.

If you need to, let the tears flow.

If at times you feel you're not heard, go and tell someone else.

In your darkest hour, pick up the phone to someone - family, friend or helpline.

It's NEVER OK to hurt yourself more than others can hurt you. ASK FOR HELP.

Chapter 2

Never be afraid to tell others what you want them to know.

Listen, and follow the advice of those who are qualified to help.

Always remember that while you're hurting inside, your closest family and friends will be hurting too.

There'll always be those who'll travel your journey with you and help you along the path.

Explain to others why their well-meaning advice sometimes just doesn't work. If you don't tell them, they won't know.

The past has an important part to play in the present and the future; if you've demons they need to be dealt with at the time.

At your lowest point, counsellors, therapists and helplines are always there to help. You talk, they listen; there's always someone available day or night. They're not there to judge, just help.

Remember to always thank those who are there for you.

Chapter 3

If you hurt someone close to you, do what you can to put it right.

If medication is suggested, talk through the reasons why and how it can help.

Understand that recovery takes time.

Do not feel guilty about your illness.

If you can't go back to your previous way of life, admit it and look at a way to move on.

Read positive, uplifting books.

If people leave, let them go.

Ring in every New Year with a promise to yourself.

Chapter 4

Take some serious time out to sit quietly; maybe learn some meditation skills.

Use some time to plan what it is you want to achieve in the immediate future.

Look inside for your intuition; listen to what it's telling you.

Be determined.

Believe in the visions and dreams you have in your mind.

Set some short-term goals to work towards – these will keep you focussed. Think of them as stepping stones across a rambling brook.

If you have a wobble day, go with the flow; it's natural and things will seem better the next day. Go to bed feeling focussed on the next day's plans and you will wake up focussed and revived.

Share your plans so family, friends and supporters will help keep you focussed on the end results and assist you with motivation to move forward.

(If you have no one close who you want to share plans with, seek out a group via local events, social media or the internet. There's always someone there to help.)

Chapter 5

Keep focused and determined.

Recognise the negative thought patterns and using positive thinking tips from others, find ways to turn them around.

If you hit a wall and fear that you're heading backwards, pick up the phone and seek help from a professional person.

Don't worry if tears fall, it's part of the recovery process now.

Share any small achievements with those who care so that you can celebrate your success.

Remember your recovery is a journey; don't let others' actions affect your way forward.

Write a gratitude list of all the good things you have in your life; read it daily.

Spend time with positive people who you care about and who care about you.

Chapter 6

Keep notes on how you're feeling and keep at whatever task is in hand to assist you reach your goals

Read and re-read books whose guidance on how thoughts become reality demonstrates a positive way to move forward.

Put into practice visualisation techniques; see your goal in your minds' eye, focus on it, give it breath and belief.

Capture your visions and dreams so they become real to you.

When you've turned a corner, be proud of yourself and your achievement.

Worry will make a panic attack worse. Just hold a vision of being calm and breathe through it.

If you're afraid of something, don't push yourself to get over it; let it be until you are ready to face the problem.

Seek help with ways to cope and lessen panic attacks.

Chapter 7

As you move through your goals take each closed action as a huge positive step towards recovery.

The bigger the goals the more clear and focussed you need to be.

Clarity is a huge key to bringing your exact thoughts to reality. Be careful what you wish for!

Discuss your future plans with trusted confidantes; by showing their belief in you it will encourage you to believe in yourself.

Whatever your plans are, there's ALWAYS somebody or an organisation that can and will help.

Every time you think of your plans, do it with a smile which will bring them energy.

Trust in you, your intuition and keep the faith

Take time to look back at your life, journey and how far you've come down the road to recovery. Be proud.

Chapter 8

Address negative thought patterns as they happen. Find a way.

Procrastinating is not good; it can lead to self-doubt.

Be strong and stand tall, hold your dream close and breathe into it.

Don't be afraid or ashamed to share your story. It surprised me how many people I met had suffered from depression and were indeed on a similar journey.

Write a list of affirmations and read them daily along with the gratitude list.

Write the affirmations in the present tense – I am, I have, I can etc.

Take time to enjoy how far you've come, and…

Again, CELEBRATE ALL ACHIEVEMENTS, however big or small.

Chapter 9

If something brings back a negative thought, go with the skid and allow it to flow through and out. Replace it with a positive.

Always focus on the future; do not allow yourself to pick up the pieces of the past.

Spend time EVERY day visualising the outcome of your goals and the future they'll provide.

Wobble days in the beginning are a fact of life; work through them. Read positive books, surround yourself with positive people and actions.

Walk tall and hold your head high; by looking at the sun it will continue to shine.

It's OK to feel a little scared; if things aren't working out the way you desired a re-think of the plan may be required.

Whatever your plans, big or small, they're your plans; always believe there's a way to make them happen

Continue to take each day as it comes; each day is a tiny stepping stone to a glorious future.

Chapter 10
CELEBRATE!

It doesn't matter how long it takes to face your fears, all that matters is that you understand that when the time is right, you will.

Allow others to help you through your fears, let them hold your hand.

If you're asked to go on the radio – just do it!

It's OK to wear wellingtons with your party dress.

Get your future visions onto a vision board, have fun and be creative with your dreams.

Attend a vision board workshop or read about how to create them. It will help you focus.

Sometimes you have to take giant leaps to make small steps forward.

Always be grateful for all the assistance and support you have been given on your life's journey.

Chapter 11

Surround yourself with the best possible positive energies; settings, people, careers and events all have a part to play.

Keep an open mind; opportunities can come into your life at any time.

Understand that the law of attraction does work for those who have an open mind to practice it.

If you want a particular outcome then visualise and feel it; a major step in making it a reality.

Be prepared to be amazed!

Love every minute of the life you're living.

Always be grateful for the experiences that life throws at you – what a great way to learn.

Remember, it's not what happens in your life but how you chose to deal with it that matters.

And So.....

At the time of starting my business I added 'Life Coaching' to its name. I've realised as time has gone on that the Awaken umbrella is constantly open to evolution, so in order to help new people though different avenues I dropped its tag and opened up its heart.

If you want to find out more about my story, my journey or the workshops Awaken can offer you in the way of inspiration, motivation and coaching (including Vision Boarding, Positive Thinking and Empowerment Events or joining your event as a speaker) please visit and get in touch at:

www.awakenlifecoaching.co.uk or at
www.beverleyjones.co.uk
'Lighting your journey ahead'

Recommended Reading Material

Love Life, Live Life – Sue Stone
The Power of your Subconscious Mind – Dr Joseph Murphy
Heal your Life – Louise Hay
The Power is Within You – Louise Hay
The Secret – Rhonda Byrne
The Magic of Believing – Claude M Bristol
The Cosmic Ordering Service – Barbel Mohr
Positively Happy – Noel Edmonds
Awakening – Elizabeth Villani

**PSYCHE
BOOKS**

The study of the mind: interactions, behaviours, functions.
Developing and learning our understanding of self. Psyche
Books cover all aspects of psychology and matters relating to
the head.